AUSTRALIA REMEMBERS 1

Anzac Day, Remembrance Day & War Memorials

ALLISON PATERSON

Little Big Sky

First published 2018
This edition published 2025

Big Sky Publishing Pty Ltd
PO Box 303, Newport, NSW 2106, Australia
Phone: 1300 364 611
Fax: (61 2) 9918 2396
Email: info@bigskypublishing.com.au
Web: www.bigskypublishing.com.au

Cover Design and Typesetting: Think Productions

A catalogue record for this book is available from the National Library of Australia

National Library of Australia Cataloguing-in-Publication entry
Author: Allison Paterson
Title: Australia Remembers 1. Anzac Day, Remembrance Day & War Memorials
ISBN: 9781925675788 (HB)

CONTENTS

Chapter 1

LIVING IN AUSTRALIA

The Australian Defence Force

The ADF consists of the Australian Army, Royal Australian Navy and Royal Australian Air Force. The three organisations once worked separately but were united as the ADF in 1976.

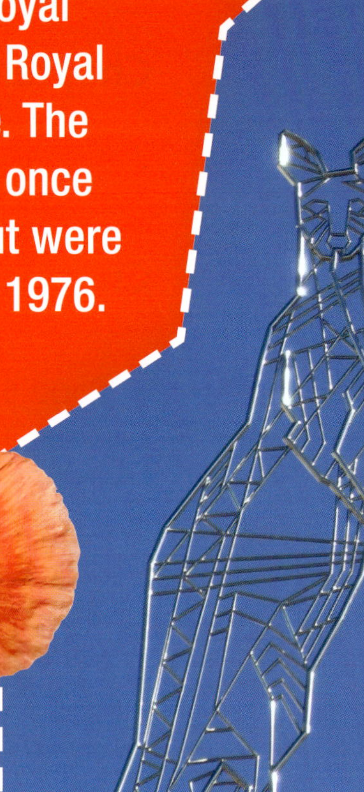

Parliament House Flag and Coat of Arms, Canberra.

Australia is a wonderful country — the people who live here are healthy, safe and free to make their own decisions. As Australians, we have the right to go to school, to choose where to live, to choose our jobs and our religion. Emergency workers such as ambulance officers, police and firefighters help to protect and care for us. Members of the Australian Defence Force (ADF) also keep us safe. The soldiers of the Australian Army, sailors of the Royal Australian Navy and airmen and women of the Royal Australian Air Force defend our country and our freedom. They also help us in times of crisis, such as when natural disasters strike.

But life can be different in other countries and, in some places in the world, there can be **conflict**. When conflict happens the leaders of countries will try to resolve it in a peaceful way. Peaceful solutions cannot always be found, and this can lead to war. The ADF also assists other people around the world who may be suffering because of conflicts, or in times of crisis.

Army, Navy and Air Force personnel of Australia's Federation Guard (courtesy Department of Defence).

Private Joshua Hetherington talks to an Afghan child in Uruzgan Province, 2010 (AWM P11170.005).

Chapter 2

COMMEMORATION

Our **servicemen and women** deserve our gratitude and respect. In Australia, we have two major days of **commemoration**, Anzac Day and Remembrance Day. On these days we honour, thank and remember all those who have fought to protect others, or suffered in war and conflicts in the past. We also recognise those who may be serving our country in dangerous places today.

Both days help us remember the sacrifice so many men and women have made for our freedom and safety. We also reflect on our country's achievements and what it means to be an Australian.

How do people show their gratitude and respect to others?

Think of some examples in your daily life.

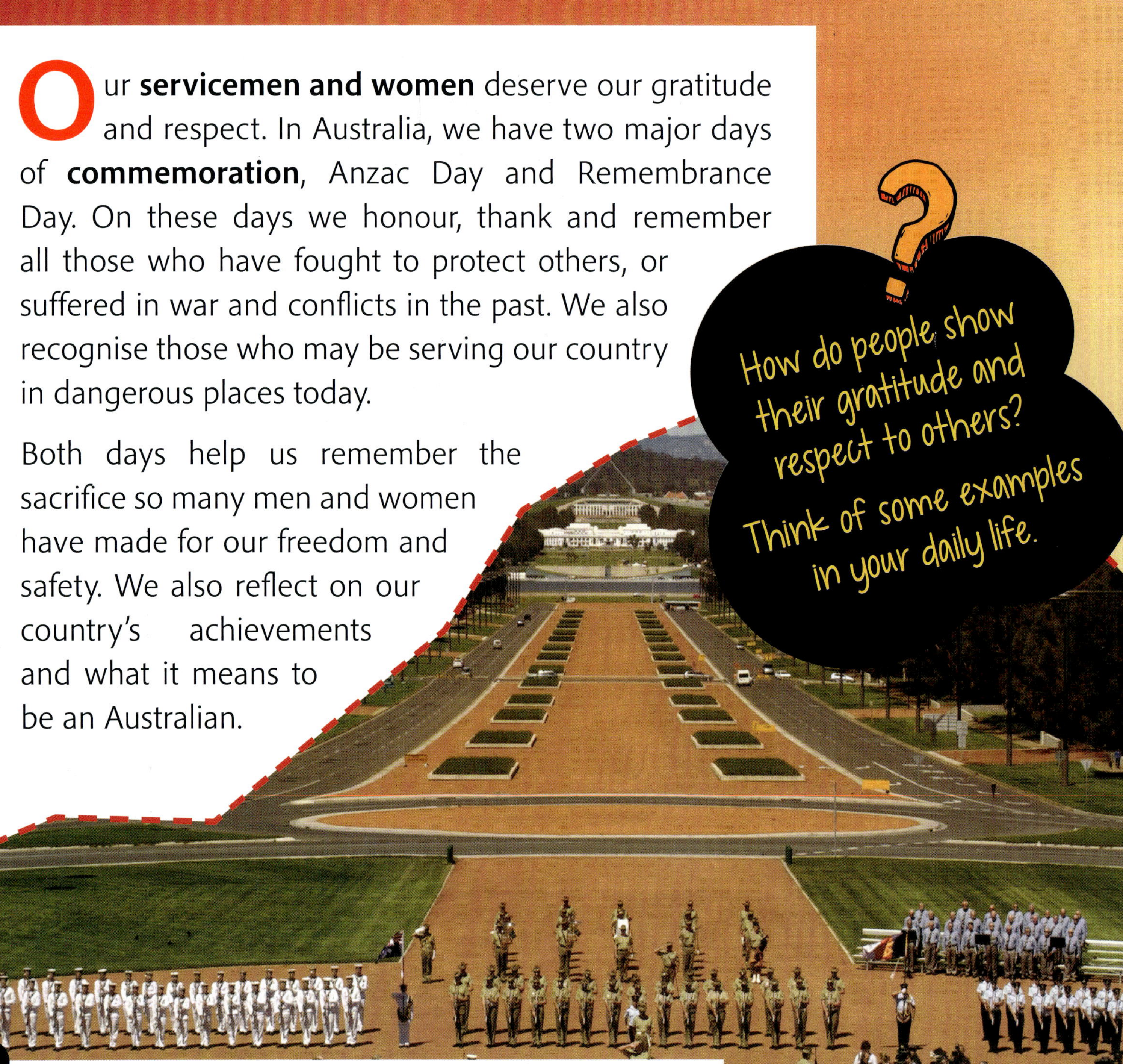

Remembrance Day service, Canberra (courtesy Department of Defence).

Anzac Day service in Peregian Springs, 2017 (courtesy St Andrew's Anglican College).

Anzac Day service in Tewantin, 2012 (courtesy St Andrew's Anglican College).

DID YOU KNOW?

Commemoration means to honour the memory of an event, a group of people or a person by holding a service, ceremony, or celebration. Special memorials or objects are also made to help us honour and remember.

Men and women sacrificed their lives so that we can live in peace with our friends and family. In the most random times I will stop and think of just how lucky we are. Lucky to be free with the ones we love, lucky to live when and where we live, and lucky to have such dedicated ancestors who fought for us.

Jacqueline (aged 14)

What started as a job as an infantry private when I was 19 has turned into a lifetime career that I have served with pride. It is not just a job - it is a duty to protect, a reason to live and a chance to make the world of my grandson a safe place to live and grow - just like our past veterans who gave their lives to allow us the chance to live in freedom and safety. It's important to understand remembrance as a way of giving thanks for our way of life today - for you never know when that will change.

Major David Hopgood,
Australian Army
(Rwanda, East Timor, Afghanistan)

Chapter 3

ANZAC DAY

Anzac Day occurs on 25 April and is an important national commemorative occasion. It is a public holiday both in Australia and New Zealand. This date was chosen as our national day of remembrance because it marks the anniversary of the day in 1915 when the **Australian Imperial Force** (AIF) and the New Zealand forces began their first major military action on the Gallipoli Peninsula during World War I. **Citizens** gather at **memorial** services, ceremonies, parades and other commemorative events. Anzac Day services are also held in countries where soldiers from Australia and New Zealand have served or are serving today.

DID YOU KNOW?

The AIF was the volunteer Australian military force that served overseas in World War I. It was known as the 1st AIF. The 2nd AIF was formed in World War II.

The earliest known photograph of troops landing at Anzac Cove, taken at around 5.30 am on 25 April 1915 (AWM P10140.004).

I will never forget the courage that the soldiers had to fight and give us a better life.

Grace (aged 11)

The Landing at Gallipoli

At 4.30 am on 25 April 1915, Australian troops began landing at Anzac Cove on the Gallipoli Peninsula in Turkey. The Allies, which included countries such as France, Russia and those of the British Empire, planned to capture Constantinople, the capital city of Turkey. At that time, Turkey was fighting on the side of the Germans. If the Allies could capture Constantinople, it would prevent the Turkish people fighting for the Germans. But the campaign was not successful. From the landing on 25 April to the time when the Australians were withdrawn eight months later, over 8,700 Australian troops were killed.

Coloured illustration of Anzac troops after the fighting at Gallipoli during World War I.

Anzac Day is a national commemorative event. What does this mean? Do you know of other commemorative events that are held in your state, local area or your school?

World War I

World War I broke out in Europe on 28 July 1914 and lasted over four years, ending on 11 November 1918. It was one of the most devastating wars in history and millions of people died. It was so bad that most people could not believe there would ever be another war. They called it 'the war to end all wars'. From a population of fewer than five million, over 416,000 Australians volunteered to serve their country in the AIF. More than 60,000 of the volunteers lost their lives. Over 3,000 Australian women volunteered as nurses, serving as members of the Australian Army Nursing Service. Twenty-five nurses died while serving overseas.

What do you know about World War I? Find out what countries were involved. Why do you think it was called a world war?

Chapter 4

THE REAL MEANING OF ANZAC

The Australian 9th and 10th Battalion tent lines at Mena Camp, looking towards the Pyramids. The soldier in the foreground is playing with a kangaroo, the regimental mascot (AWM C02588).

ANZAC is an **acronym** that stands for the Australian and New Zealand Army Corps. The acronym was first used in 1915 when soldiers from both countries were training together in Egypt. The soldiers became commonly known as 'Anzacs' while serving at Gallipoli. Over time, the acronym became the word 'Anzac'. The word is significant to both Australia and New Zealand, and is used not only as a name for soldiers, but also for a set of positive values, or spirit. It is also used to name buildings, parks and memorials and even as a name for biscuits.

Anzac Cove

The ANZAC troops landed on a beach on the Gallipoli Peninsula on 25 April 1915. The narrow beach became a busy port and headquarters for the Corps. The commander of the Corps was General Sir William Birdwood. He decided to name the beach 'Anzac Cove' to honour the bravery of the Anzacs. Anzac Cove is visited by large numbers of people every year who pay their respects to the first Anzacs at the cemeteries and memorials on the Gallipoli Peninsula.

Mustafa Kemal

Colonel Mustafa Kemal was one of the Turkish commanders at Gallipoli who fought against the Anzacs. He became the first President of the Republic of Turkey in 1923. He was named 'Ataturk' — 'father of the Turks' — in 1934. His words appear on a memorial on the Gallipoli Peninsula and also at Anzac Parade in Canberra:

> Those heroes that shed their blood and lost their lives …
>
> You are now lying in the soil of a friendly country. Therefore rest in peace. There is no difference between the Johnnies and the Mehmets to us where they lie side by side here in this country of ours …
>
> You, the mothers, who sent their sons from faraway countries wipe away your tears; your sons are now lying in our bosom and are in peace, after having lost their lives on this land they have become our sons as well.
>
> Ataturk, 1934

Is the word Anzac used on any landmarks in your local area?

Memorial at Anzac Cove featuring the words of Mustafa Kemal (Ataturk) in a speech made in 1934.

After Gallipoli, the Australians served in the Middle East and on the Western Front in France and Belgium. Thousands more men enlisted in the AIF. They continued to serve with the same spirit as the original Anzacs. But many more lives were lost as the war continued for the next three years.

DID YOU KNOW?

The main area of fighting in Western Europe in World War I was called the Western Front. It was a network of trenches stretching from the English Channel in Belgium, through France to the border of Switzerland. It was approximately 750 kilometres long.

> *Anzac stood, and still stands, for reckless valour in a good cause, for enterprise, resourcefulness, fidelity, comradeship and endurance that will never own defeat.*
>
> C.E.W. Bean (1946)

The charge of the 4th Light Horse Brigade at Beersheba on 31 October 1917. This photograph is possibly a later re-enactment of the charge, but some claim that it came from a Turkish camera captured on the day (AWM P03723.001).

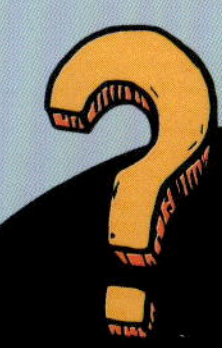

Using a world map, locate the countries where Australians served in World War I, including Turkey (Gallipoli), Egypt, Syria, Palestine, France and Belgium.

Why would Australians want to fight in a war so far away from home?

The Western Front and the Middle East

Australian soldiers arrived on the Western Front in France and Belgium in early 1916. They were involved in many battles and suffered heavy casualties. Close to 47,000 Australians died at places including Pozières, Fromelles, Bullecourt, Passchendaele, Villers-Bretonneux, Hamel and Mont St Quentin. The Australian Light Horse troops served on the Sinai Peninsula of Egypt, and in Palestine and Syria. These countries form part of a large area of north-east Africa and western Asia known as the Middle East. Over 4,000 Australians lost their lives in battles throughout the Middle East at locations such as Romani and Beersheba.

Tyne Cot Cemetery, Belgium. This memorial shows the cross of sacrifice and headstones which are all the same, regardless of rank, as no one soldier was more important than another.

Sergeant J. Holland and Sergeant J. Fulton carry a wounded man through the mud to a dressing station near Lae, New Guinea, 1943 (AWM 015787).

Charles Bean and the AIF

Charles Bean was a journalist who became Australia's official war correspondent. He thought Australian soldiers were very brave and he admired the way they looked after their mates. After the war he founded the Australian War Memorial so that the men of the AIF would never be forgotten.

In our family, my mum's uncle went to fight in a war. He was very brave and won lots of medals for bravery and kindness. He still looks after his mates and their families even after the war has finished.

Noah (aged 7)

DID YOU KNOW?

A legacy can be anything handed down from one person or group to another. It could be personal property that an ancestor hands down, or a tradition or an idea that comes from the past.

The Anzac Spirit

Australian soldiers displayed courage, mateship, resourcefulness, endurance and sacrifice. These character strengths became known as the 'Anzac spirit', a legacy which is an important part of our national identity. Australians are proud of the Anzac spirit; it has helped to form our traditions, our culture and our thoughts on what it means to be an Australian.

What does the Anzac spirit mean to you? Can you think of times when you or someone you know has shown the qualities of the Anzacs?

Mateship

The Australian soldiers of World War I were known for their spirit of comradeship, which Australians call 'mateship'. The concept of mateship began during the early years of Australian settlement when convicts and settlers needed to rely on one another for help. The Australian soldiers inherited these characteristics from their ancestors. The experiences of the soldiers created a deep bond and respect for others. Most believed that everyone is equal, that no-one is better, or has more rights than anyone else. Many enjoyed a joke and playing pranks. Most of all, they were loyal and prepared to make great sacrifices to help a mate.

The 'Cobbers' statue at the Australian Memorial Park at Fromelles, France.

Why would it be important to the Anzacs to have great mates? Think about your own friendships, do you display the qualities of being a good friend to others?

Diggers

Australian and New Zealand soldiers who served in World War I were also known as 'diggers'. This word was first used in Australia to describe the miners during the gold rush years of the 1850s. People from all over the world rushed to Australia hoping to find gold. The Anzacs began to use the word 'diggers' in 1916–17 when they were digging the trenches and fighting on the Western Front. 'Digger' or 'dig' is used in the same way as the word 'mate' and Australian and New Zealand soldiers are still called 'diggers' today.

Men of the 53rd Battalion waiting to don their equipment for the attack at Fromelles, July 1916 (AWM A03042).

Chapter 5

ANZAC DAY SERVICES, CEREMONIES AND PARADES

Anzac Day Begins

Anzac Day was first commemorated over 100 years ago in 1916. Services and parades were held in Australia, New Zealand, London and on the Western Front in France and Belgium where soldiers from Australia and New Zealand were serving. A sports competition was also held in Egypt. In Sydney, wounded soldiers and nurses attended a parade at which large crowds waved and cheered. These events encouraged more men to enlist in the AIF.

The Catafalque Party presents arms during an Anzac Day service at Lone Pine, Gallipoli.

Anzac Day commemorates all Australian Defence Force personnel who gave their lives fighting for freedom. No-one owns Anzac Day, it belongs to all Australians … Australians are dedicated even more to the freedom they have because of the sacrifice of others.

Sergeant Kevin O'Halloran,
Australian Army (Rwanda)

The Australian Flag

The flag is an important Australian symbol which represents our history, identifies us as Australian and gives us a sense of pride in our nation. A flag is lowered to half-mast as a sign of remembrance and respect for those who have lost their lives.

Australian flags placed by visitors at Pozières, France.

Since then, on 25 April each year, the people of Australia and New Zealand have continued to reflect, remember and show gratitude for those who have been affected by war.

After World War I there were mixed feelings about Anzac Day. Some soldiers wanted to forget their tragic experiences of war and did not attend the events. Many felt it should be a time of solemn commemoration, while others wanted to celebrate the important contribution Australians made to ending the war. Anzac Day became both, with services, ceremonies and parades in the morning and social events for returned soldiers, such as reunions, in the afternoon.

By 1927, every state of Australia had decided that Anzac Day would be a public holiday and by the mid-1930s the traditions we know today had become part of our culture.

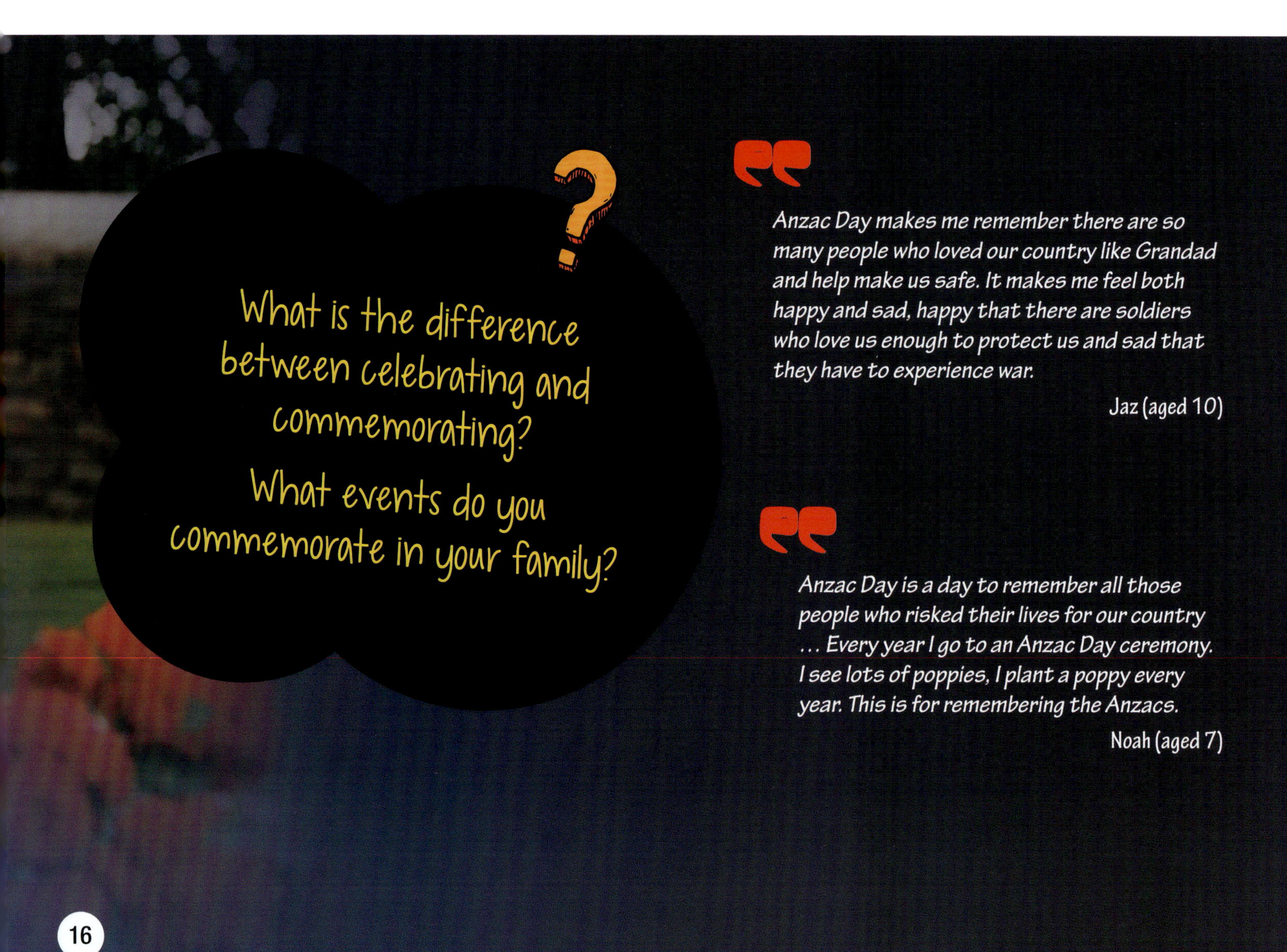

What is the difference between celebrating and commemorating?

What events do you commemorate in your family?

Anzac Day makes me remember there are so many people who loved our country like Grandad and help make us safe. It makes me feel both happy and sad, happy that there are soldiers who love us enough to protect us and sad that they have to experience war.

Jaz (aged 10)

Anzac Day is a day to remember all those people who risked their lives for our country ... Every year I go to an Anzac Day ceremony. I see lots of poppies, I plant a poppy every year. This is for remembering the Anzacs.

Noah (aged 7)

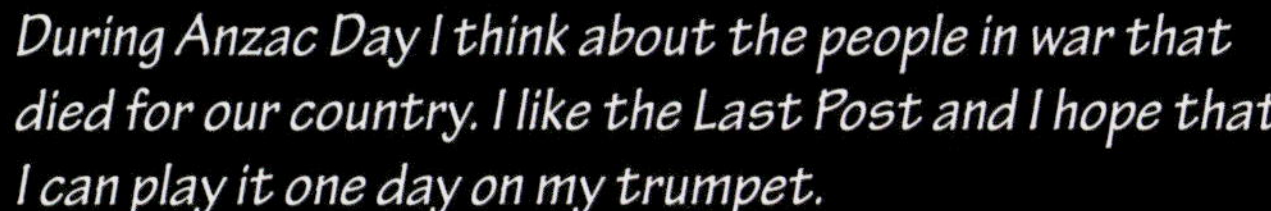

During Anzac Day I think about the people in war that died for our country. I like the Last Post and I hope that I can play it one day on my trumpet.

Joshua (aged 9)

The Bugle Calls

The bugle has been used by Army buglers for many years to play tunes that have different meanings for the soldiers. During Anzac Day and Remembrance Day services you will hear three kinds of bugle calls:

- The **Last Post** signals the end of the day. In the commemorative service it is a final farewell, a sign that the dead soldiers have done their duty, and now they can rest peacefully.
- The **Rouse** is played during a daytime service. It signifies that, after a period of **mourning** (sadness for the dead), our life and duty will continue.
- **Reveille** marks the beginning of the day and is sounded at a dawn service in place of the Rouse.

An Australian bugler plays The Last Post at VC Corner Cemetery, France (courtesy Department of Defence).

The Dawn Service

The dawn service on Anzac Day is a tradition in Australia and New Zealand. It marks the time of day when the first Anzacs landed at Gallipoli. It is also a symbol of the mateship soldiers felt as they woke before daylight in the front-line trenches and prepared to defend their positions, a practice called 'stand-to'.

There are different views on when the first dawn service was held as many were organised by churches or individuals. The first 'official' dawn service is thought to have been at the memorial **Cenotaph** in Sydney.

A Bren gunner from the 1st Battalion, Royal Australian Regiment stands-to on the front line, Korea, 1953 (AWM HOBJ3883).

DID YOU KNOW?

The word cenotaph means 'empty tomb'. It is a monument built to honour those killed in war but who are buried elsewhere.

When I stand shivering in the cold, as the sun rises during the Anzac Day service, I reflect on how scared and brave the soldiers were going in to battle. With their sacrifices I have been blessed to live out my tomorrows.

Jack (aged 13)

Anzac Day dawn service at Monument Hill, Fremantle, in Western Australia (courtesy Department of Defence).

The Earliest Dawn Services

Reverend Arthur Ernest White held a ceremony in 1914 for the soldiers who were departing in the first convoy of ships that left from Albany, Western Australia. The service was held at 4.00 am. Reverend White later served as a chaplain on the Western Front during World War I. In 1929 he returned to Albany as the minister of a local church and, a year later, he held a dawn service at his church. During his service, he promised those soldiers who had died that: 'As the sun rises and goeth down, we will remember them.'

A church service was also held at dawn in Albany in 1918 and at Toowoomba, Queensland, in 1919.

DID YOU KNOW?

The word **veteran** can have different meanings, such as working for a long time in a job. It can also have different meanings in the defence force. Sometimes it refers to people who have actively fought in a war, while at other times the word **veteran** refers to any person who has served in the armed forces.

The Dawn Service Window at Forbes, New South Wales (courtesy Australian Army History Unit).

Wreaths adorn the base of the Sydney Cenotaph after an Anzac Day dawn service (courtesy Department of Defence).

The sun rises over the Anzac Day dawn service at Anzac Cove. (courtesy Department of Defence).

Early in the morning of Anzac Day in 1927, a group of returned soldiers (veterans) came across a lady placing a **wreath** at the construction site of the Sydney **Cenotaph**. The veterans decided they would arrange a dawn service there the following year. By 1935 the number of people attending the service at Sydney had grown to 10,000 and dawn services were being held in the capital cities of every state and in many towns across Australia.

Symbols and traditions play an important part in Anzac Day services and parades, as well as other commemorative events. Many of these have interesting stories. Can you think of any symbols or traditions that you have noticed on Anzac Day?

The way I spent Anzac Day this year was attending my first dawn service and laying a wreath. I commemorate Anzac Day for all Anzacs, not just the ones that passed away during war. I also commemorate my great-grandpa who is still living. He was in the Navy in World War II.

Sophie (aged 11)

World War II

But World War I was not the 'war to end all wars' after all, and another major world conflict began in 1939 and lasted until 1945. It was called World War II. In 1943, the Anzac Day services and ceremonies also included those who were currently serving or had lost their lives in World War II.

Over time, the number of people attending Anzac Day services and parades decreased, particularly as many of the soldiers of World War I passed away. Some people thought that Anzac Day was a celebration of war rather than a way to commemorate the sacrifices made.

In the 1980s, descendants of veterans were permitted to march in the parades. They were proud of the service of their ancestors. Immigrants from other nations who had fought for the same cause as Australia were also encouraged to march, as were children who represented their schools.

Cameron Baird VC MG, medal set.

Medals and Honours

Members of the ADF are awarded medals for their service during times of conflict. They can also receive medals which honour acts of bravery during battle. Servicemen and women wear their own medals on their left side over their heart. Family members, or those wearing medals which are not their own, wear the medals on their right side.

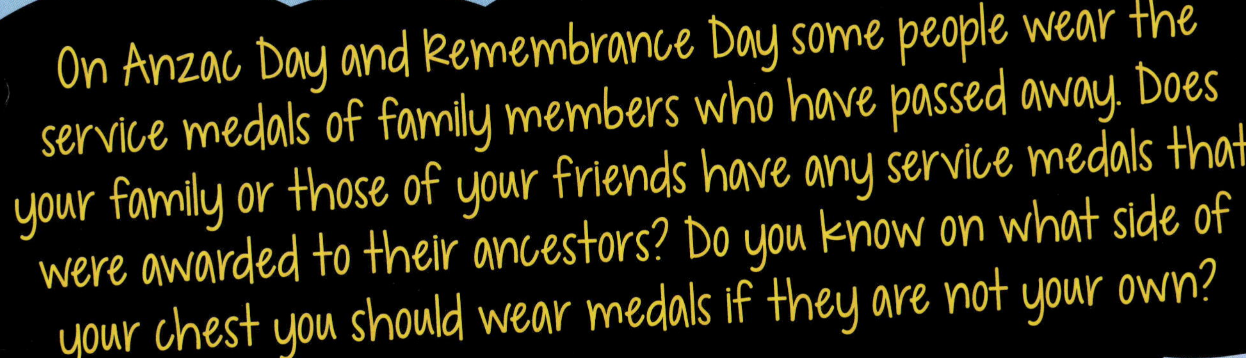

Rosemary

Rosemary is a herb often used in cooking and is also an emblem of remembrance across the world. Since ancient times people have thought that it improves memory. Rosemary was very significant to the Anzacs. It grew wild at Gallipoli and it is thought that soldiers used rosemary to decorate the graves of those who had died. Sprigs of rosemary are worn on Anzac Day.

I get teary when I think of two people who fought for Australia in World War I and World War II. One of these people was my great-great-uncle who fought in World War II. He died in Papua New Guinea. In World War I my great-great-grandfather was lucky because he survived Gallipoli and was able to come back to Australia to have a family. So Anzac Day and Remembrance Day mean a lot to me because one part of my family ended while another part kept going. I love my great-great-uncle and great-great-grandfather dearly.

Naomi (aged 10)

Anzac and Remembrance Days are about sharing memories with someone else who's been through warfare … you cannot talk about it to those who haven't experienced it.

Lieutenant Commander Tom Lewis OAM, RAN (Iraq)

Today, Anzac Day helps us to remember all those from the ADF who have served Australia in wars, conflicts, or on **peacekeeping** missions.

The number of people who attend an Anzac Day dawn service at memorial locations across Australia is continuing to grow. The services are usually organised by the Returned and Services League of Australia (RSL) or other community groups.

Anzac Day service in Bendigo, 2015 (courtesy Boyd Robertson, Bendigo RSL).

Schoolchildren laying a wreath on Anzac Day (courtesy of St Andrew's Anglican College).

I am a young /old veteran of the Vietnam War (83 years old) and this year … I led my troops in the Sydney march from a wheelchair … The march was enthusiastically supported by large Sydney crowds along the whole route, which our soldiers enjoyed immensely.

Colonel Ian Barry Mackay, Australian Army (Vietnam)

Veteran selling badges for the RSL in Bendigo (courtesy Boyd Robertson, Bendigo RSL).

The Returned and Services League of Australia (RSL)

The RSL is an organisation that helps serving and past members of the ADF. The RSL began in 1916 as the Returned Sailors and Soldiers Imperial League of Australia. It was set up by wounded or sick servicemen returning from World War I. The veterans wanted to ensure that the friendship and support they experienced while they were serving would continue.

The RSL helps to organise Anzac Day and Remembrance Day services across Australia and continues to support war veterans and their families. They also provide care packages to ADF members who are serving overseas.

DID YOU KNOW?

Servicemen and women are often asked to form a peacekeeping force to serve in countries where there is conflict. Peacekeepers can help negotiate peace agreements and ensure they are maintained. They aim to prevent violence, provide medical help, they can teach others and help to rebuild important structures like roads, schools and hospitals.

Soldiers on patrol in Afghanistan (courtesy Department of Defence).

Why would attendance at Anzac Day services be growing? Can you imagine how a veteran might feel on Anzac Day? How do you feel?

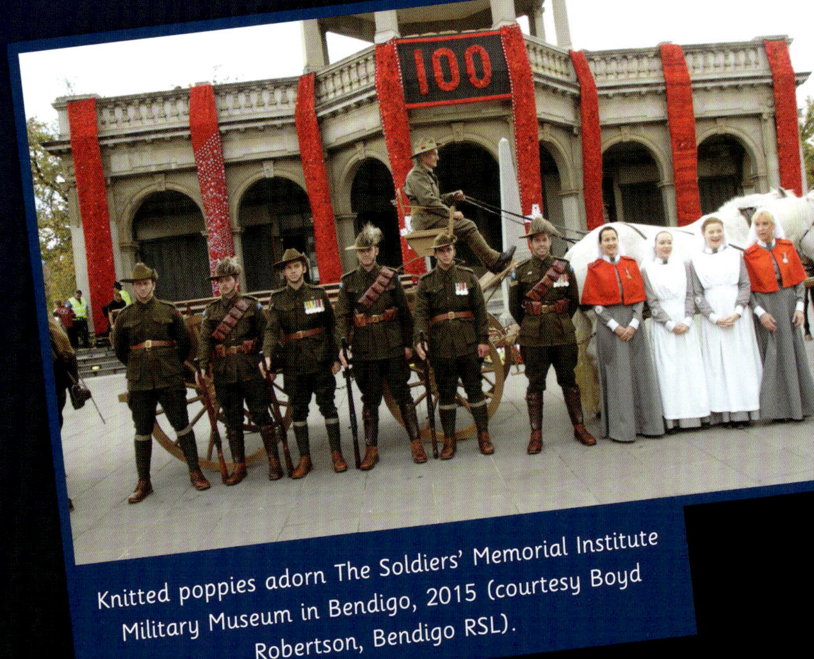

Knitted poppies adorn The Soldiers' Memorial Institute Military Museum in Bendigo, 2015 (courtesy Boyd Robertson, Bendigo RSL).

Legacy

Legacy is a charity that assists the family members of servicemen and women who lose their life, are wounded or are injured during or after their service to Australia. Legacy began after World War I to help care for the dependants of veterans. Legacy members (volunteers called 'Legatees') believe that the government has a responsibility to ensure families are provided with the care they need. They see this as a legacy of the service of the veteran. Legacy helps children with their education, provides financial assistance and supports families through tough times.

Anzac Day is one of quiet contemplation on the sacrifice of good friends lost, taken too young in the prime of their lives. I see their bright faces still, the verve they had for life, of the values they lived, of their unswerving loyalty and friendship, and their readiness to step up when times were tough. I think of the loss to our nation of so many fine young men who put their country's needs before their own, and say a silent prayer for them.

Brigadier Chris Roberts AM, CSC, Australian Army (Vietnam)

The Anzac Centenary

Over 100 years have now passed since the beginning of World War I. Across the world, between 2014 and 2018, there were services and parades held to remember this centenary. In 2015 Australia also commemorated the Anzac centenary which marked 100 years since the first Anzacs landed at Gallipoli. We honoured and remembered the 102,000 Australians who have given their lives while serving Australia in the past century. Special services and events were held, new memorials were built, and original ones were restored both in Australia and in other countries. Australians found new ways to remember, including the development of websites, online activities and mobile applications in which stories of the service of Australians were shared.

Anzac Day centenary commemorative service in Bendigo, 2015 (courtesy Boyd Robertson, Bendigo RSL).

Anzac Day 2018, Australian National Memorial, Villers-Bretonneux, France.

Investigate how your local area commemorated the Anzac centenary. Were new memorials built?

Chapter 6

ANZAC DAY SOCIAL EVENTS

Australians not only commemorate the sacrifice of those who have served their country at services, ceremonies and parades, they also remember and celebrate the Anzac spirit at social and sporting events across the country. Some people fly the Australian flag, have picnics or make Anzac biscuits. It is a day of great national pride.

For many families it is a tradition to make Anzac biscuits on 25 April. Recipes have sometimes been passed down from one generation to another. Would you like to try baking a batch and storing them in a tin? Perhaps you can start the tradition in your own family.

Anzac Day is a special day for Australians to thank ... [those who] have gone off to war ... I thank all the soldiers that have gone before me and those after me.

Warrant Officer Class 2 Gordon Traill, Australian Army (Iraq)

Chef Scott Smith, RAN, pulls Anzac biscuits from the oven aboard HMAS Newcastle during a tour of the Middle East (courtesy Department of Defence).

Anzac Biscuits

During World War I, family members and friends at home would send parcels of supplies such as soap, socks, writing paper, fruit cakes and biscuits to the soldiers and nurses who were away at the war. It could take two months or even longer for a soldier to receive a parcel as all mail travelled by boat. The biscuits, which were also known as the 'Soldiers' Biscuit', were made from oats, flour, sugar, golden syrup and coconut. They were popular because they stayed fresh for a long time and were often packed in used tins. Today many families and schoolchildren make Anzac biscuits on Anzac Day.

Anzac Day Football

The soldiers of World War I loved to play different types of football. In recent times there have been special matches on Anzac Day afternoon, with both Australian Rules football and Rugby League matches played. Since 1995 the Anzac Day Clash has been played between the Australia Football League teams of Collingwood and Essendon. Two National Rugby League teams, the Sydney Roosters and the St George Illawarra Dragons, have contested the Anzac Day Cup since 2002. A commemorative service is held before each game.

The 1st Australian Convalescent Depot rugby team, Le Havre, France, 1918.

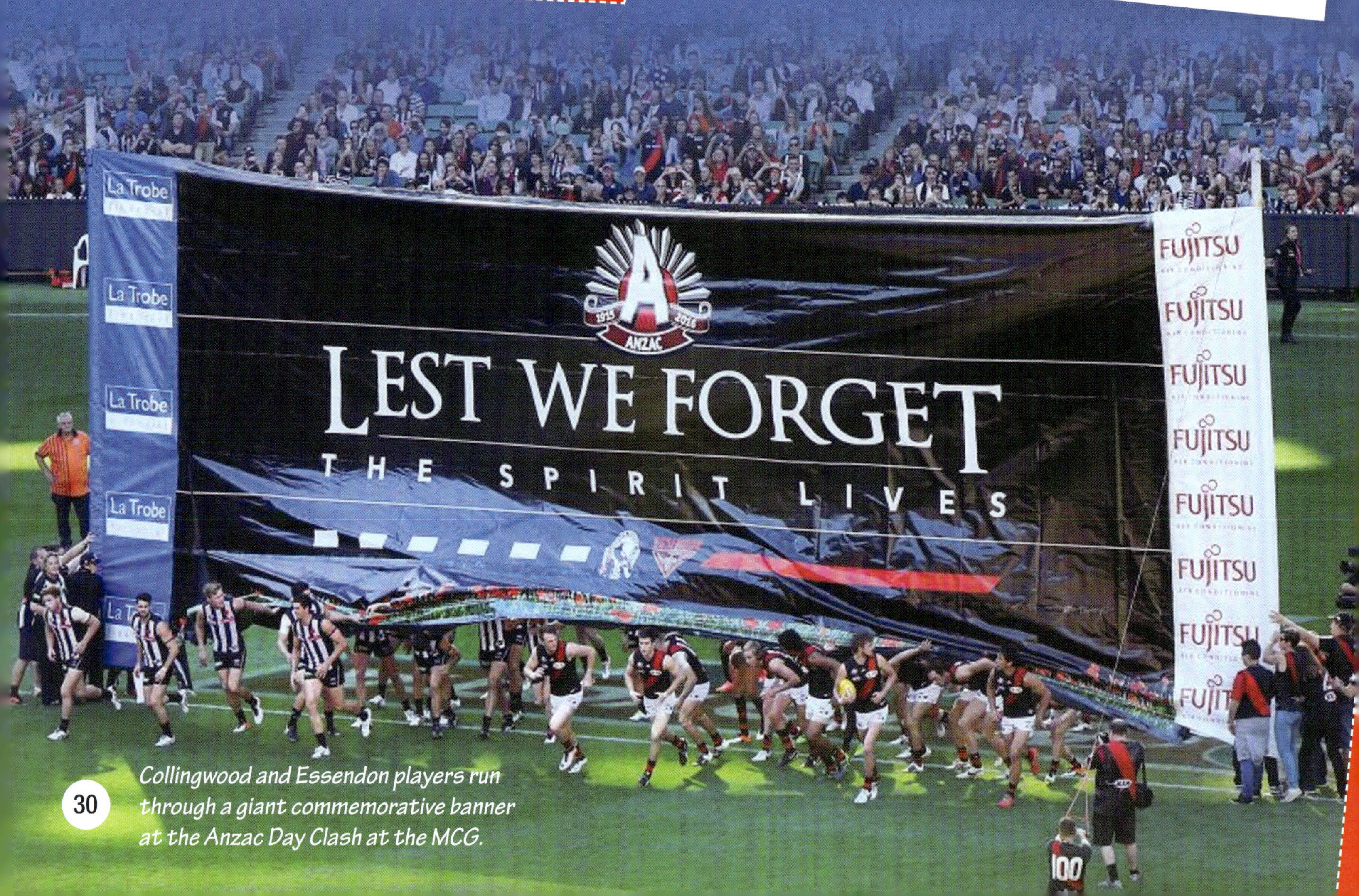

Collingwood and Essendon players run through a giant commemorative banner at the Anzac Day Clash at the MCG.

Are there events held in your local community after Anzac Day services and parades?

Two-up

Two-up is a game of chance that was very popular with Australian soldiers. Two or three coins, usually pennies (which are no longer part of Australia's currency) are placed on a piece of wood called the 'kip' and then tossed in the air. The person who tosses the coins is called the 'spinner'. Players try to guess how the coins will land. Will two heads or two tails land facing up? Or will there be a head and a tail? Two-up is traditionally played after Anzac Day services in places like RSL clubs.

Two-up kip and coins (courtesy Australian Army History Unit).

A group of Australian soldiers plays two-up behind the ruins at Ypres, Belgium, in 1917 (AWM E01199).

Chapter 7

REMEMBRANCE DAY

Officers at le Havre, France on the day the Armistice was signed, 11 November 1918.

The Memorial at the Armistice Clearing at Compiègne, France, 2014.

Remembrance Day

Remembrance Day occurs on 11 November and is marked by memorial services and ceremonies in Australia and in many other countries across the world such as Canada, the United Kingdom, New Zealand, the United States, France and Belgium. Like Anzac Day, this commemorative day began because of the events of World War I. The eleventh hour of the eleventh day of the eleventh month marks the time in 1918 when the **Armistice** was signed to declare a ceasefire. It was signed at 5.00 am with all fighting to stop at 11.00 am.

DID YOU KNOW?

An armistice is an agreement or truce between countries at war to stop the conflict and discuss conditions for peace. Once the conditions have been agreed by both sides, the agreement becomes known as a peace treaty.

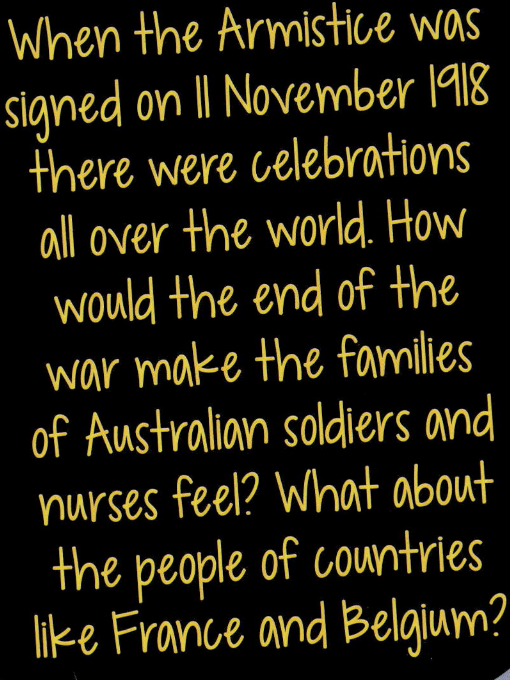

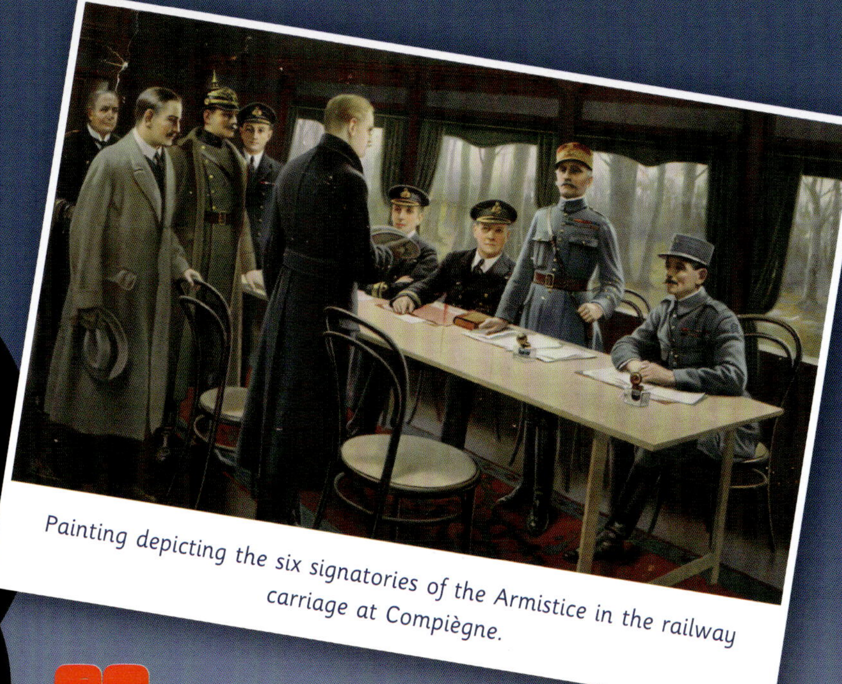

Painting depicting the six signatories of the Armistice in the railway carriage at Compiègne.

> *Remembrance Day for me signifies 'the war to end all wars' and the end of World War I. So many didn't return from Gallipoli and the Western Front, a tragic waste of life. I remember all of those that didn't return to their families and friends.*
>
> Warrant Officer Class 2 Gordon Traill, Australian Army (Iraq)

Some of the thousands of Australian schoolchildren who knitted socks for the men at the front. A heap of socks is visible at the centre of the photograph (AWM H11581).

Today people honour and thank those who fought and died in wars and conflicts to protect the rights and safety of people in countries across the world. We remember all members of the supporting services of the armed forces, the families who lost loved ones, refugees who lost their homes, those who returned to rebuild their lives and those who support the efforts of others to bring peace. People who are suffering today because of war are also remembered.

Do you know of any countries in the world that are not peaceful like Australia? Perhaps you, or a friend or family member has come to live in Australia from a country that is not safe. If so, what does Remembrance Day mean to you?

It is not only the veterans from well-known conflicts that patriotically served their country that I pause to remember. It is the varied lives that were touched by war — the nurses, families and friends of those that went to war, for they either came home changed or they didn't come home at all.

Major David Hopgood, Australian Army (Rwanda, East Timor, Afghanistan)

Matron Grace Wilson at the 3rd Australian General Hospital on Lemnos Island, May 1915 (AWM A05332).

Refugees are people who have been forced to flee their country because it is not safe to stay there. This could happen in times of war or conflict.

Remembrance Day to me, and especially the observation of a minute's silence, is especially moving. Anyone that knows the futility and violence of war will attest to how 'loud' that silence must have been in 1918, when the guns finally fell silent on the Western Front. It was meant to be the war that ended all wars. I use the time to think of those that never came home from the 'Great War' and I remember my own friends who have paid the ultimate sacrifice since.

Major Bram Connolly DSM, Australian Army (Somalia, Timor, Afghanistan)

The First Remembrance Day

The first Remembrance Day occurred in 1919 and was known as Armistice Day. People paused at 11.00 am, stood in silence, and remembered for two minutes. The name of Armistice Day was changed to Remembrance Day during World War II. In 1997 the Governor-General of Australia, Sir William Deane, officially recognised 11 November as Remembrance Day. He recommended that all Australians observe one minute of silence at 11.00 am.

The Silence of Respect

In both Anzac Day and Remembrance Day services we stand in silence to respect and remember those who have given their lives in the service of their country. This ritual began on 11 November 1919. An Australian journalist, Edward Honey, had written to a London newspaper in 1919 suggesting five minutes of silence should be observed on Armistice Day. Sir Percy Fitzpatrick, a South African, also suggested that a period of silence should occur in all countries of the British Empire. King George V liked the idea and decided that everyone should stop in a 'complete suspension of all our normal activities' for two minutes at 'the eleventh hour of the eleventh day of the eleventh month'. Trains and cars even stopped as a sign of respect.

All traffic stops and service personnel stand to attention during the two minutes' silence on Armistice Day in Melbourne, 11 November 1942 (AWM 137060).

There have been many wars and conflicts since World War I and we remember and honour the sacrifices made by those who have fought and continue to fight in wars as they serve our country. People do this by attending a Remembrance Day service at a church, a war memorial, school or other appropriate locations. We also remember by observing a period of silence at 11.00 am or wearing a red poppy. It is a time to remember those who sacrificed their lives, to be grateful we live in peace and to think about others who may not have the same freedom and safety that Australians enjoy.

Lest We Forget

The words 'lest we forget' often appear on war memorials and are also said during commemorative services and ceremonies. These words mean 'we must not forget' and they are a promise that we make never to forget the sacrifices others have made for the life we have today.

Students place poppies during a school service (courtesy St Andrew's Anglican College).

The Ode of Remembrance

In September 1914, in the early days of World War I, a man named Laurence Binyon wrote a poem called 'For the Fallen' to help people remember the soldiers who had died in the war. We use part of that poem today at Anzac Day and Remembrance Day services to help us remember:

They shall grow not old, as we that are left grow old;
Age shall not weary them, nor the years condemn.
At the going down of the sun and in the morning
We will remember them.

The people attending the service then repeat:

We will remember them.

Lest we forget.

When I remember our soldiers from past wars, I feel as if I am part of their tradition and that I am honouring the courage and bravery of those who served our country and who wore a uniform like mine. I feel as if I am one of them.

Major Catherine McCullagh, Australian Army

Students wearing poppies on Remembrance Day 2015 (courtesy St Andrew's Anglican College).

Lieutenant Colonel John McCrae in uniform

Chapter 8 POPPIES

***In Flanders' Fields the poppies blow
Between the crosses, row on row...***

Poppies are a symbol of remembrance and respect across the world. They commemorate those who gave their lives in war. Poppies grew wild on the battlefields of France and Belgium, and at Gallipoli. They also grew in the cemeteries where wooden crosses marked the graves of those who died.

The First Poppies of Remembrance

In 1918, Moina Michael, an American woman working for the Young Men's Christian Association (YMCA), read the poem 'In Flanders' Fields' and chose to write her own poem called 'We Shall Keep the Faith'. Moina described red poppies as a symbol of the blood of the soldiers who died in the war. She decided to always wear a red poppy. Madame Guérin, who worked for the French YMCA, suggested that artificial poppies be made and sold. The money raised was used to help ex-servicemen, war widows and their children.

The poppy became the international memorial flower to be worn on Armistice Day. Poppies were first sold on 11 November 1921 and the Returned Sailors and Soldiers Imperial League of Australia (later the RSL) bought one million poppies to sell. Some of the money raised went to France to help the children who had suffered because of World War I.

12ft high sculpture of 'Poppies' in the town of Amiens, France.

Field of poppies

'In Flanders' Fields'

Lieutenant Colonel John McCrae was a medical officer in the Canadian Army in World War I. In 1915, near the town of Ypres in Belgium, he wrote a poem he called 'In Flanders' Fields'. It became one of the most famous poems of the war. McCrae died of an illness in January 1918 and was buried in France. The poem is usually read as part of a commemorative service:

In Flanders' fields the poppies blow
Between the crosses, row on row,
That mark our place; and in the sky
The larks, still bravely singing, fly
Scarce heard amid the guns below.
We are the Dead. Short days ago
We lived, felt dawn, saw sunset glow,
Loved, and were loved, and now we lie
In Flanders' fields.

Take up our quarrel with the foe:
To you from failing hands we throw
The torch; be yours to hold it high.
If ye break faith with us who die,
We shall not sleep, though poppies grow
In Flanders' fields.

Try making your own poppy. Turn to the back of this book for instructions.

The wearing of a single poppy is a sign that we remember the sacrifices made to keep us safe and protect our way of life. We lay wreaths made of poppies or other flowers on Anzac Day during memorial services. Poppies are also used at other times to show our respect and gratitude at war cemeteries and memorials such as the Australian War Memorial.

The original cross placed over the grave of George Marlow who died of his wounds on 21 September 1917.

George Marlow's headstone today.

Poppies left at George Marlow's headstone.

Every year on Anzac Day I attend a dawn service. I wear a poppy which has become a symbol of war remembrance the world over. It is a time for me to reflect and say thank you to those that fought in a war and for the men and women who are still serving today.

Lieutenant Commander Debbie Dunchue, Royal Australian Navy

Chapter 9

WAR MEMORIALS ACROSS AUSTRALIA

War Memorials

War memorials are created to remember all those who were wounded or died in war. They can commemorate individual people, groups of people or a conflict. People of other countries also create their own war memorials. There are many different types and they can be buildings, monuments, statues, gardens, **plaques**, avenues of honour, honour boards, stained-glass windows, even street names and swimming pools. Often the names of the men and women who died are listed on a war memorial.

A memorial stone and plaque (courtesy St Andrew's Anglican College).

Ballarat Arch of Victory, Victoria.

Anzac Memorial Hyde Park, Sydney.

When I was a child, my parents told me stories about their service in the Air Force during World War II. It wasn't until I was serving in the Air Force that I understood the importance of those stories — the importance of remembering those who have served and sacrificed for our nation. By commemorating the brave women and men who have gone before us, we have the opportunity to learn from their bravery and how we can continue the work they so courageously started.

Squadron Leader Patricia McDonell, Royal Australian Air Force

Shrine of Remembrance, Victoria.

The Shrine of Remembrance – Melbourne, Victoria

The Shine of Remembrance is the Victorian state memorial to Australian servicemen and women. It was designed and built by veterans of World War I and opened in 1934. A ray of natural light shines through a slot in the roof and beams down on the commemorative stone at 11.00 am on the eleventh day of the eleventh month each year, at the precise time when the Armistice was signed in 1918 — the day that is now known as Remembrance Day.

Benalla Methodist Church Pioneers Stained Glass Windows, Victoria.

Wesley Uniting Church World War I Roll of Honour, Dubbo, New South Wales.

World War I Memorials

After World War I, individuals and communities all over Australia wanted to commemorate those who had fought or suffered in the conflict. Fundraising events were held in towns and cities to raise money to build memorials which still exist today.

In 1920 a war memorial was constructed at a small town in northern Victoria called Mologa. Lieutenant Allan Marlow and his twin brother, Private Percy Marlow, had returned to their family at Mologa in 1919. Three of their brothers were killed on the Western Front. When the memorial was finished, Allan Marlow and his mother unveiled it as the people of the town gathered around to remember all those who had died. The town of Mologa no longer exists, but residents of the local area still hold services at the memorial on Anzac Day and Remembrance Day.

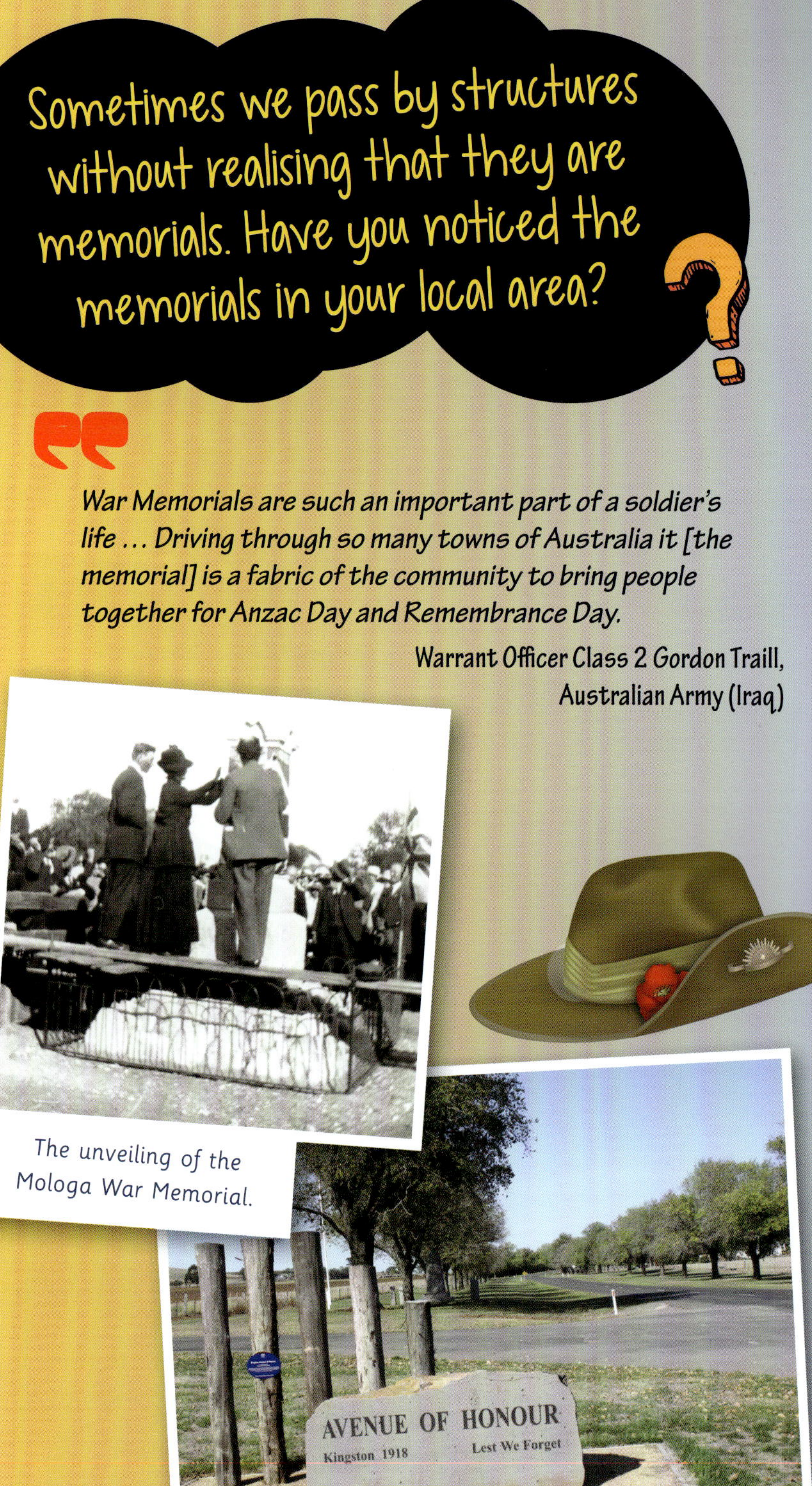

Sometimes we pass by structures without realising that they are memorials. Have you noticed the memorials in your local area?

War Memorials are such an important part of a soldier's life … Driving through so many towns of Australia it [the memorial] is a fabric of the community to bring people together for Anzac Day and Remembrance Day.

Warrant Officer Class 2 Gordon Traill, Australian Army (Iraq)

The unveiling of the Mologa War Memorial.

The Avenue of Honour in Kingston, Victoria.

I feel very proud of my ancestors at the Anzac Day ceremony at Mologa. They fought hard to make a peaceful Australia for kids like me. I will always be grateful and say thank you by learning more about them and making sure Mologa is not forgotten about in my family.

Thomas (aged 8)

The house which Allan Marlow built and named 'Passchendaele'.

Individuals also created their own memorials. Allan Marlow built a home of mud bricks which he made himself. Above the front door he placed a stained-glass window with the word 'Passchendaele', the name of a village in Belgium and a battle in which he and his brothers had fought. Allan had built his own memorial to his brothers and the mates he lost during the war.

Anzac Day is important to me to help remember those people who gave up their lives for their country ... it is a day of respect for those who went to war. I go to Mologa each year because I have two great-uncles from there who went to war. One of these uncles did not come home. He did not get to grow old.

Maddy (aged 10)

Pyramid Hill Memorial Hall, Victoria.

Memorials all over Australia have been built at different times to remember service groups, people, or conflicts that have happened since World War I.

Does your family commemorate ancestors on Anzac Day or Remembrance Day?

If you are not sure, find out if you have ancestors who have served or suffered in a war.

The Great Ocean Road in Victoria, which was built by returned servicemen after World War I. It opened in 1932 and is a lasting memorial to those who gave their lives.

Kings Park Cenotaph, Perth, Western Australia.

Australian Flying Corps and Royal Australian Air Force Memorial, Mildura, Victoria.

National Memorial, Adelaide, South Australia.

Australian Service Nurses Memorial, Anzac Parade, Canberra, ACT.

World War II Memorials

World War II broke out in 1939 after Germany invaded the countries of Poland and Czechoslovakia. Almost one million Australians served in places including Germany, Italy, Greece, Africa, Singapore, Papua New Guinea and East Timor. Just as in World War I, memorials to those who gave their lives and those who suffered during World War II were created to commemorate the sacrifices made.

On Anzac Day and Remembrance Day, we remember our great-grandad and his friends who fought in World War II. Every year we love hearing stories about him flying his Spitfire plane, dressing up in his uniform and wearing his medals in the Anzac parade to remember what he did for our family and country.

Cooper (aged 10) and Ryder (aged 8)

Darwin Cenotaph, Northern Territory.

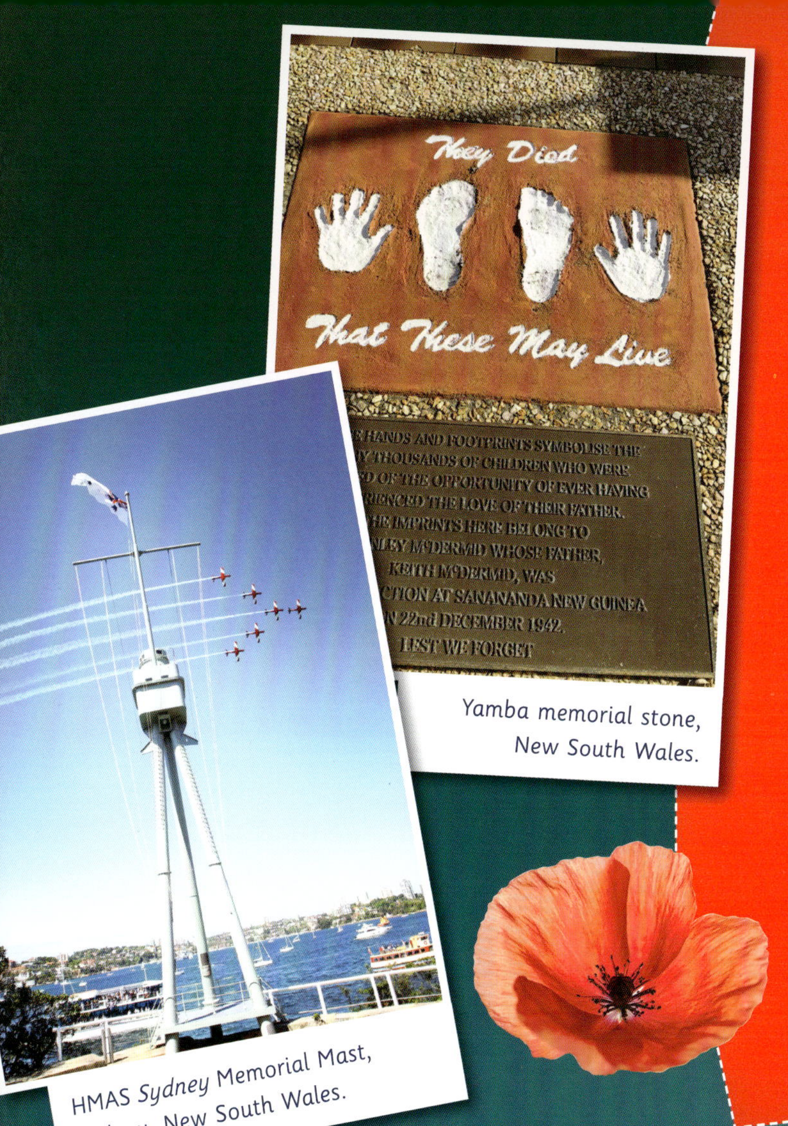

Yamba memorial stone, New South Wales.

HMAS *Sydney* Memorial Mast, Sydney, New South Wales.

Australia in World War II

Australia was threatened by Japanese forces in 1942 and Australian servicemen in Singapore became prisoners of war. Australian nurses also were imprisoned or lost their lives as they tried to escape the Japanese forces. The city of Darwin in the Northern Territory was bombed several times, the first raid occurring on 19 February 1942. Japanese air raids also hit Broome in Western Australia and other places along the northern Australian coastline, as well as Townsville and parts of north Queensland. Japanese midget submarines were sunk in Sydney Harbour on 31 May and submarine attacks occurred along the east coast for several months afterwards. Over 30,000 Australian servicemen were captured during World War II and 39,000 Australians lost their lives. The war ended in 1945 after Germany surrendered on 7 May, followed by the surrender of Japan on 2 September.

Remembering Since World War II

After World War II, Australian servicemen and women served, and have continued to serve during conflict in countries such as Korea, Malaya, Vietnam, Iraq and Afghanistan. Members of the ADF have been sent as peacekeepers to countries such as Rwanda, Somalia, East Timor and Solomon Islands when conflict broke out. They have also helped people in Australia, Indonesia and other countries following events such as natural disasters.

Australia's coastline still has the remains of constructions, such as lookouts, which were built to protect our country during World War II. In your local area, or in places you have visited, is there any evidence of the time when Australia was under threat?

The National War Dog Memorial was erected at Alexandra Headland in Queensland in 2001. Originally, it was a memorial for the 11 tracker dogs that served the Australian Army during the Vietnam War. Plaques have since been added which honour dogs involved in other conflicts.

Peacekeeping 1947 – today

Australians have been involved in international peacekeeping for more than 70 years, with the first mission to Indonesia in 1947. Since then, Australian peacekeepers have served in more than 60 peacekeeping operations in countries and regions of the world such as Indonesia, Kashmir, the Middle East, Cyprus, Iran, Iraq, Zimbabwe, Namibia, Cambodia, Somalia, Rwanda, Western Sahara, Bougainville, East Timor and Solomon Islands. Sixteen Australians have died while serving as peacekeepers.

The pipers' lament during a memorial service for those who died in the Battle of Long Tan on 18 August 1966. This service was held at Long Tan in South Vietnam on 18 August 1969, the first anniversary of the battle (AWM BEL_69_0556_VN).

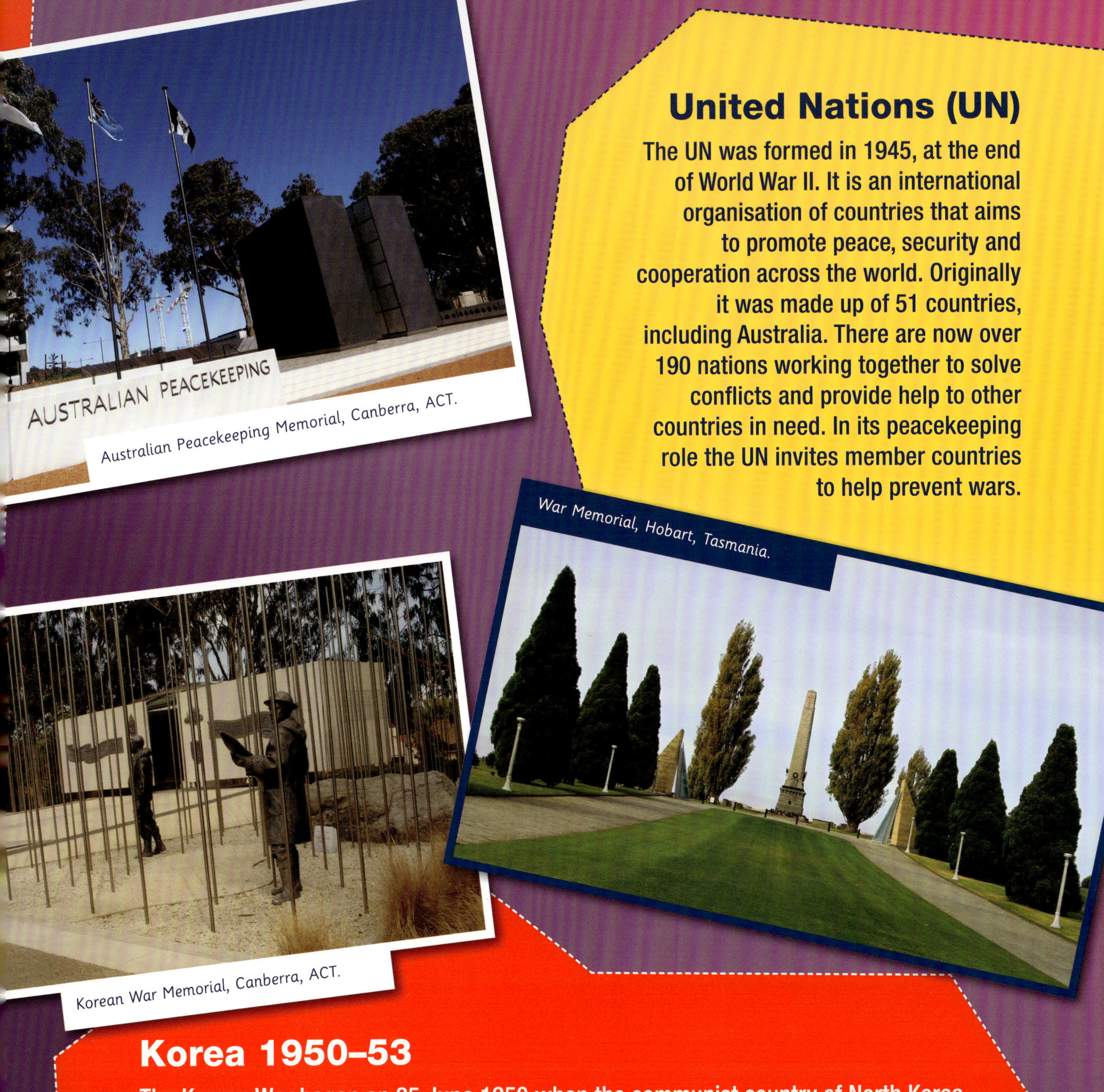

Australian Peacekeeping Memorial, Canberra, ACT.

War Memorial, Hobart, Tasmania.

Korean War Memorial, Canberra, ACT.

United Nations (UN)

The UN was formed in 1945, at the end of World War II. It is an international organisation of countries that aims to promote peace, security and cooperation across the world. Originally it was made up of 51 countries, including Australia. There are now over 190 nations working together to solve conflicts and provide help to other countries in need. In its peacekeeping role the UN invites member countries to help prevent wars.

Korea 1950–53

The Korean War began on 25 June 1950 when the communist country of North Korea invaded South Korea. Communism is a way of ruling a country which was feared in many nations because it restricts personal wealth, rights and freedoms. Australian forces supported South Korea as part of a larger UN force. An armistice was signed on 27 July 1953 but not before 340 Australians had lost their lives and more than 1,200 had been wounded. North Korea and South Korea remain divided today.

Malayan Emergency 1948–60 and Indonesian-Malaysian Confrontation 1963–66

The Malayan Emergency began in 1948 because of communist activities in that country. Australia became involved in 1950. The Emergency ended in 1960, but Australians remained in Malaya (Malaysia today) until 1963. Thirty-nine Australian servicemen died while serving in Malaya.

Between 1963 and 1966 Australia helped to defend the new Federation of Malaysia. The neighbouring country of Indonesia began raids on Malaysia in 1963. Australian and British forces helped to protect Malaysia until a peace treaty was signed in 1966. Sixteen Australians died during the Confrontation.

Australian Navy Memorial, Canberra, ACT.

Aboriginal War Memorial at Burleigh Heads RSL, erected in 1991.

Vietnam 1962–73

In 1954 Vietnam was divided into South Vietnam and North Vietnam. The communist leader of North Vietnam wanted to control the whole country. South Vietnam was supported by the United States of America (USA) which wanted to stop the spread of communism. Australia, New Zealand, the USA and South Vietnam fought against North Vietnam.

From 1962 to 1973 over 60,000 Australians served in Vietnam. More than 500 died there and around 3,000 were wounded. In 1973, the Australian combat servicemen and women came home and in 1975 North Vietnam took control of the country.

Afghanistan 2001–ongoing – The War on Terror

Afghanistan is a country that has seen much conflict and, after the terrorist attacks on the USA in 2001, it was discovered that terrorist groups were secretly training in Afghanistan. Australians had died in the terrorist attacks on the USA in 2001 and in Bali, Indonesia, in 2002. In 2001 Australian military service personnel joined forces with the USA to help stabilise Afghanistan to prevent the training of terrorists and attempt to combat terrorism across the world.

The war in Afghanistan is one of the longest wars in which Australia has been involved. Forty-one Australians have been killed in action and more than 260 have been wounded. In 2018 Australian servicemen and women remain in Afghanistan assisting and training its citizens and helping to reduce the influence of terrorist groups.

Iraq 1990–91 – The War on Terror 2003-09

The ADF has been involved in two conflicts in the country of Iraq in recent decades. The first occurred in 1990 when Iraq invaded the neighbouring country of Kuwait on 20 August. Australian forces and defence personnel from other countries helped to free Kuwait on 24 February 1991.

The USA was attacked by terrorists in 2001 and the President declared a 'war on terror'. Iraq was thought to be supporting terrorists and to have weapons of mass destruction. Australian, British and American forces invaded Iraq on 20 March 2003 and quickly overthrew Iraq's brutal leader. No weapons of mass destruction were found. Australians remained in Iraq until July 2009 to help prevent a civil war and to train Iraqi soldiers.

Australian Vietnamese War Memorial Brisbane, Queensland.

Afghanistan Memorial, Canberra, ACT.

Russia
Norway
Sweden
Estonia
Latvia
Lithuania
Belarus
Denmark
Ireland
United Kingdom
Germany
Poland
Ukraine
France
Czechia
Slovakia
Austria
Hungary
Moldova
Romania
Switzerland
Croatia
Serbia
Bulgaria
Italy
Spain
Portugal
Greece
Turkey
Georgia
Armenia
Azerbaijan
Kazakhstan
Uzbekistan
Turkmenistan
Kyrgyzstan
Tajikistan
Afghanistan
Pakistan
Iran
Iraq
Syria
Lebanon
Cyprus
Israel
Jordan
Kuwait
Qatar
U.A.E.
Saudi Arabia
Oman
Yemen
India
Nepal
Bhutan
Bangladesh
Myanmar
Tunisia
Morocco
Algeria
Libya
Egypt
Mauritania
Mali
Niger
Chad
Sudan
Eritrea
Burkina Faso
Guinea
Sierra Leone
Liberia
Côte d'Ivoire
Ghana
Togo
Benin
Nigeria
Central African Rep.
South Sudan
Ethiopia
Somalia
Cameroon
Gabon
Congo
Democratic Republic of Congo
Uganda
Kenya
Rwanda
Burundi
Tanzania
Comoros
Angola
Zambia
Malawi
Zimbabwe
Mozambique
Madagascar
Namibia
Botswana
eSwatini
Lesotho
South Africa
Atlantic Ocean
Indian Ocean
World War I
1914–1918*
1 German New Guinea
Bitapaka
2 Turkey
Gallipoli, Anzac Cove, Krithia, Lone Pine, The Nek, Hill 60, Hill 971
3 Sinai
Romani, Rafa, Magdhaba
4 Palestine
First and Second Gaza, Beersheba, Es Salt, Megiddo, Abu Tellul, Nablus, Ammon, Kaukab
5 Mesopotamia
Kurna, Kut el Amara, Baghdad, Ramad, Damascus
6 Egypt/Cyrenaica
Um Rakhum, Gebel Medwa, Halazin
7 France
Somme, Fromelles, Pozieres, Mouquet Farm, Bullecourt, Villers-Bretonneux, Hamel, Amiens, Mont St Quentin, Montbrehain, Gueudecourt, Lagnicourt, Hebuterne, Dernancourt, Hazebrouck, Morlancourt, Lihons, Proyart, Hindenburg Outpost Line, St Quentin Canal
8 Belgium
Messines, First Ypres, Passchendaele, Menin Road, Polygon Wood, Broodseinde, Poelcappelle
9 Azerbaijan
Baku
10 *Russia – Russian Civil War, 1917-1923
Emptsa
Colonial Sec
Eureka Stockade, 18
New Zealand - Maori
Sudan, 1885
Burma - Hmawang, 1
South Africa - Boer
Belmont, Graspan, S
Paardeberg, Coetze
Wilmansrust, Driefo
Koster River, Stinkh
Onverwacht

1945 to Present

1. **Korea - Korean War, 1950-1953**
   Yong ju, Kapyong, Maryang San, Samichon River, Sariwon, Ku jin, Pakchon
2. **Malaya - Malayan Emergency, 1948-1960 and Confrontation, 1962-1966**
   Sungei Bemban, Sungei Siput, Sungei Kesong, Sungei Koemba, Kindau, Babang
3. **Vietnam War, 1962-1972**
   Gang Toi, Long Tan, Ap My An, Coral-Balmoral, Binh Ba, Long Khanh
4. Israel 1956 to present
5. Egypt 1981 to present
6. Somalia, 1993
7. Rwanda, 1994-1995
8. East Timor, 1999 to 2013
9. Afghanistan, 2001 to present
10. Iraq, 2003 to present
11. Solomon Islands, 2000 to 2013
12. Sudan, 2011 to present
13. North-west Australia, 2004 to present

World War II 1939-1945

1. **North Africa**
   Bardia, Tobruk, El Alamein, Derna, Giarabub, Er Regima, Mechili, Ruin Ridge, Tel el Eisa
2. **Greece**
   Vevi Pass, Brallos Pass, Tempe Gorge
3. **Crete**
   Retimo, Heraklion
4. **Syria**
   Litani River, Damour, Merd jayoun, Damascus
5. **Malaya**
   Gemas, Jemaluang, Singapore, Bakri
6. **Papua New Guinea**
   Rabaul, Kokoda Track, Milne Bay, Buna-Gona, Wau, Lae, Salamaua, Sattelberg, Shaggy Ridge,Wewak, Slater's Knoll, Sananando, Mubo, Kaiapit, Finschhafen, Keppel Harbour
7. **Netherlands East Indies**
   Ambon,Timor,Tarakan (Borneo),Balikpapan (Borneo), Labuan-Brunei Bay

North Korea
South Korea
Vietnam
Philippines
Brunei
Malaysia
Sarawak
Borneo
Indonesia
Java
Timor
Timor-Leste
Papua New Guinea
Solomon Is.
Pacific Ocean
Fiji
Australia
New Zealand

Find the locations around the world where Australians are serving today.

We must not forget the new generation of veterans, not only the younger veterans from war in the Middle East, but the peacekeepers. Those of Somalia and Rwanda — just young soldiers going to Africa to help another nation and yet in doing so, have to live with the ramifications of those warlike situations and the trauma of what they were unprepared to see and do. Many lives are changed as a result of serving your country. Veterans do this as they are full of national pride and good intentions. They deserve their actions to be remembered.

Major David Hopgood, Australian Army (Rwanda, East Timor, Afghanistan)

What do peacekeepers do? Why is it important to help others?

Has there been a natural disaster in your community when members of the ADF have arrived to help?

Chapter 10

THE AUSTRALIAN WAR MEMORIAL

The Australian War Memorial in Canberra was opened on 11 November 1941, during World War II. This national memorial had its beginnings in 1917. Captain Charles Bean was Australia's official **war correspondent** and **historian** during World War I. After seeing the great sacrifices and achievements of the Australian soldiers and nurses during the war, he suggested that Australia should create a national memorial. The collection of items from the war began in 1917.

Australian War Memorial, Canberra, ACT.

Australian War Memorial, Canberra, ACT.

Here is their spirit, in the heart of the land they loved; and here we guard the record which they themselves made.

Charles Bean

Captain Charles Edwin Woodrow (C.E.W.) Bean

Charles Bean was born in Bathurst, New South Wales, on 18 November 1879 and became a journalist. When World War I broke out he was appointed official war correspondent and historian. He landed at Gallipoli on 25 April with the Anzacs, remaining at Gallipoli throughout the campaign even after he was wounded in August. He also served on the Western Front, staying until the Armistice was declared. He returned to Australia in 1919. It took him 23 years to write six of the 12-volume official history. He died in 1968.

In 1948 Charles Bean explained why he was so determined that Australia should have its own war memorial, dedicating it to those who had given so much for Australia during the war:

> Here is their spirit, in the heart of the land they loved; and here we guard the record which they themselves made.

While built as a memorial to all those who have served Australia, or suffered during wars or conflicts, the Australian War Memorial has two other important roles. It is a museum in which war relics are displayed and also an **archive** where important documents and items from past wars are kept and preserved.

In 2015, during the centenary of the Anzac landing at Gallipoli, over 1.14 million people visited the Australian War Memorial. Today, more than 120,000 students visit each year from schools across Australia.

Charles Bean (AWM A05389).

Anzac Parade from the Australian War Memorial in Canberra, ACT. In the distance is Old Parliament House, and behind that is the new Parliament House.

Tomb of the Unknown Australian Soldier

Between nine and thirteen million soldiers from all over the world were killed during World War I. There are many cemeteries in which Australian soldiers are buried, especially in France and Belgium and at Gallipoli. Around one third of the soldiers who died were never found and have no known grave. The tombstone of an unknown Australian soldier from World War I is usually inscribed with the words:

An Australian soldier of the Great War
Known Unto God

On 11 November 1993, on the 75th Anniversary of the Armistice, an unidentified Australian World War I soldier was taken from Adelaide cemetery near the town of Villers-Bretonneux in France to the Australian War Memorial. In a speech at the memorial that day, the Australian Prime Minister at that time, Mr Paul Keating, said: ‘He is all of them and he is one us.’

Other memorials throughout the world also contain the tomb of an unknown soldier. These include Westminster Abbey in London and the Arc de Triomphe in France.

Tomb of the unknown soldier.

I remember my two relatives who fought in the world wars. I am proud of how they gave up everything for their country, how they risked their lives and risked never seeing their families again. I had the privilege of going to the War Memorial and presenting a few words to the unknown soldier … They fought for everyone, and I will never forget.

Evony (aged 12)

Entombment of the unknown Australian soldier 1993 (AWM PAIU1993_198_28).

Have you or anyone you know visited the Australian War Memorial? If so, what was your most memorable moment?

The Australian War Memorial is one of the most visited places in Australia. Why is this?

In the Australian War Memorial, the silence gave me time to reflect on my great-grandparents who fought in World War II. It made me proud and sad to think about how the war changed not only their life but others in their generation. And then I felt grateful for living in a peaceful time and I wish that it was the same for them.

I am in awe every time I visit the Australian War Memorial as it is such an amazing space to pay your respect … much more than just a building …

Warrant Officer Class 2
Gordon Traill, Australian Army (Iraq)

Tomb of the unknown soldier.

Chapter 11

AUSTRALIAN WAR MEMORIALS AROUND THE WORLD

War cemeteries and memorials exist in countries all over the world. These commemorate the great loss of life and suffering which the people of that country endured because of wars or conflicts. Often these memorials also honour the people of other nations who came to assist that country when it needed help, including Australian servicemen and women.

Many memorials were created to commemorate and honour the Australian soldiers and nurses of World War I and World War II. Today these war memorials are important to their descendants who may travel long distances to visit the last resting place of their ancestors and to commemorate the service of their family members.

I reflect, honour and remember about the men and women who made the ultimate sacrifice and served for the freedom of this great country of ours especially my own family sacrifices. To my best mate Scotty, I shall remember you for the good times, he shall not grow old … Lest we forget.

Corporal Dave Morgan, Australian Army (Vietnam)

Several memorials were erected on the plateau overlooking Kokoda village, near the start of the Kokoda Trail.

Kokoda Trail (Track) and Memorial

Japanese forces invaded the island of New Guinea to the north of Australia during World War II. Australian soldiers fought many battles against the Japanese across New Guinea, including what was then the Australian territory of Papua. In July 1942, Japanese troops landed at Buna on the shores of Papua and tried to cross the rugged terrain of the Owen Stanley Range to capture the capital of Port Moresby. Kokoda was a small village almost midway along the track which ran between Buna and Port Moresby. Many Australians lost their lives in the jungles as they battled the Japanese troops. Kokoda was recaptured on 2 November 1942.

The Kokoda Trail is also sometimes called the Kokoda Track. Over 5,000 Australians walk nearly 100 kilometres along the rough track through thick jungle every year. They do this to honour the courage, endurance, mateship and sacrifice of the Australian soldiers who fought there. These qualities of the Anzac spirit are expressed in words inscribed on the memorial at Isurava near Kokoda which was unveiled in 2002.

The Isurava Memorial, Papua New Guinea.

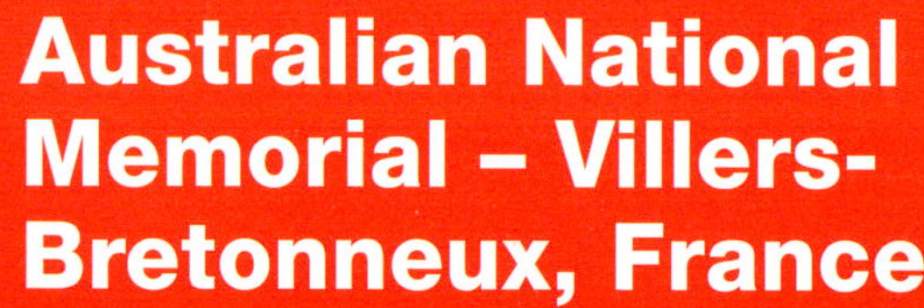

Australian National Memorial – Villers-Bretonneux, France

Villers-Bretonneux was chosen as the site for Australia's national memorial to Australian soldiers and nurses who served on the Western Front and to those who lost their lives. It was unveiled in 1938. Australian and British soldiers freed the village of Villers-Bretonneux from enemy forces on 25 April 1918. The village had been destroyed, but was rebuilt after the war with the assistance of donations from the Australian public. To mark the centenary of the Armistice, a new museum was built at the site of the memorial and was opened in 2018. It is called the Sir John Monash Centre after the Australian general who commanded the Australian Corps in 1918.

Why do people travel such long distances to other countries to visit war graves and memorials?

Villers-Bretonneux School, France.

The Wall of Remembrance at the Australian National Memorial outside Villers-Bretonneux (courtesy Department of Defence).

Villers-Bretonneux School, France.

> When the Australians came to France, the French people expected a great deal of you ... We knew that you would fight a real fight, but we did not know that from the very beginning you would astonish the whole continent ... I shall go back tomorrow and say to my countrymen, I have seen the Australians, I have looked in their faces, I know that these men will fight alongside of us again until the cause for which we are all fighting is safe for us and for our children.
>
> Georges Clémenceau, French President, 7 July 1918

The Australian Naitonal Memorial at Villers-Bretonneux including the newly completed Sir John Monash Centre (courtesy Department of Defence).

Cross of Sacrifice, Australian National Memorial, Villers–Bretonneux, France.

Chapter 12

THE LEGACY TO REMEMBER

Individuals today remember the service of their ancestors in many ways. They attend commemorative services and parades at which they may wear the medals presented to their family members. Some travel to countries across the world to visit the graves of those who died while serving, or wear a poppy, a sprig of rosemary or an Anzac badge. Others write songs and books, create an artwork or bake Anzac biscuits. Australians are both proud of, and grateful for the service of their ancestors and that of other Australian servicemen and women.

One hundred years on, it is not simply a matter of chance that Australia is a safe and prosperous country. Members of the ADF have continued to fight for our freedom in the century that has passed with the same courage, sense of mateship and loyalty of the first Anzacs.

The spirit of the soldiers of World War I lives on in the legacy they left behind. We are the custodians of that legacy and we should never forget.

Poppies, Australian War Memorial, Canberra, ACT.

DICKINSON
DOHERTY
DONALD
DONOVAN
DOYLE
DRYDEN H. T.
DUFF R. W.
DUKE F.
DUTTON A. E.
DUTTON G. A.
ERICKSON W. E.
FAIRWEATHER
FISHER
FORBES
MALKIN C. W.
MANNING W. J.
MANNING W. R.
MARSHALL B. C.
MARTIN B. N.
MASTERS A. E.
MATHESON R. L.
MAXWELL W.
MAYNARD G. M.
MEADER T. A.
MELDRUM L. R.

Chapter 13

ACTIVITIES

Make A Poppy

You need:

- Red paper – crepe paper works well.
- Black paper
- A green pipe cleaner
- Scissors
- Craft Glue

Now to make your poppy:

1. Trace or copy two poppy shapes onto your red paper.
2. Cut around the poppy shapes.
3. Cut a small circle from the black paper the size of the circle shown.
4. Make a tiny cut in the centre of each poppy shape.
5. Take a pipe cleaner and twist it slightly about 2cm from the end.
6. Push the poppy shapes onto the 2cm end until they reach the twist.
7. Arrange the poppy shapes so they overlap but not exactly on top of each other.
8. Bend the 2 cm end flat against the poppy.
9. Glue the black circle into the centre.

Your poppy is complete!

Make Anzac Biscuits

Ingredients

- 1 cup flour
- 1 cup coconut
- 1 cup rolled oats
- ¾ cup brown sugar
- 125g butter
- 2 tablespoons golden syrup
- 2 tablespoons water
- 1 teaspoon bicarbonate of soda

Anzac Biscuits

Method

1. Preheat oven to 180°C/160°C fan-forced.
2. Stir through flour, oats, sugar and coconut in a bowl.
3. Combine the butter, golden syrup and water in a saucepan and heat until the butter melts. Remove from the heat and stir in the bicarbonate of soda. (Hold saucepan over the bowl of the flour mix in case it flows over as the bicarbonate of soda bubbles up).
4. Pour the butter and syrup mixture in with dry ingredients and mix until it comes together as a dough.
5. Roll dough into small balls and place onto a greased tray ensuring that they are evenly spaced. They can be pressed down gently with a fork.
6. Bake the biscuits for about 15 minutes, or until golden brown. Remove from oven and allow to cool.

Create a Poppy Wreath

You need:

- A large round paper plate (white)
- Red paper – craft paper works best for a wreath
- Black paper
- Green paper
- Scissors
- Craft Glue

Now to make your poppy wreath:

1. Write your own Anzac Day or Remembrance Day message in the middle of the paper plate.
2. Trace or copy the poppy shape on page 62 onto your red paper.
3. Cut around the poppy shape.
4. Cut a small circle from the black paper the size of the circle shown on page 62.
5. Glue the black circle into the centre of your poppy.
6. Repeat steps 2 – 5 until you have enough poppies to cover the outer edge of the plate. The number of poppies needed will depend on the size of the plate.
7. Trace the leaf shape onto the green paper and cut. Repeat 6 times.
8. Glue your poppies and leaves onto the outer edge of the paper plate as shown in the diagram.

Creating a War Memorial

Memorials to those who served in war are found in most Australian communities. They come in all shapes and sizes and are erected to honour those who have served in war, remind us about our past, help us reflect on our way of life and provide a place for people to gather as a community to show gratitude and respect.

Look through the images in this book and consider the many different types of war memorials — from buildings, shrines, statues, memorial stones and honour boards, to avenues of honour and stained-glass windows. Personal memorials are also created in ways such as framing the medals and photos of a serviceperson, or creating a book or webpage about their life and service.

Create a design for a war memorial. It could commemorate all those who have served Australia and have suffered because of war, or be a memorial for an individual, a family member or ancestor.

When designing a memorial think about these questions:

- What materials will you use? Rocks, plants, plaques, a webpage or poster paper?
- What symbols or emblems will you include that acknowledges the service of Australians? The rising sun emblem, the Australian flag, a cross, rosemary, poppies, the Coat of Arms?
- You can include words that reflect your respect and gratitude. Include phrases and words such as:
    - Lest We Forget
    - In Loving Memory
    - Honour
    - Legacy

Where are the war memorials in your local area? What wars do they commemorate? Do they include the names of people? Are there any surnames that you know today?

- How will it reflect your local community, or family today?
- If your memorial is for public display you will need approval for the use of the following emblems:
    - The Army emblem: https://www.army.gov.au/our-work/protecting-australian-army-emblems
    - The Navy emblem: http://www.navy.gov.au/protecting-royal-australian-navy-badge
    - The Air Force emblem: https://www.airforce.gov.au/displays/requesting-air-force-displays
    - The Commonwealth Coat of Arms: https://www.pmc.gov.au/government/commonwealth-coat-arms
    - Additional information can also be found here: https://www.australia.gov.au/about-australia/facts-and-figures/national-symbols

To find out more about the customs and traditions surrounding Anzac Day, Remembrance Day and war memorials look for the next book in this series: *Australia Remembers: Customs and Traditions of the Australian Defence Force.*

GLOSSARY, INDEX & BIBLIOGRAPHY

Glossary

Acronym – a word formed from the first letters of each word in a phrase.

Archive – a place in which public records or historical materials are kept.

ANZAC – Australian and New Zealand Army Corps, an acronym representing the combined Australian and New Zealand forces who fought at Gallipoli in 1915.

Campaign – military plans and combat actions that aim to resolve a conflict.

Centenary – the 100th anniversary of an event.

Citizens – official members of a country or people who live in a particular place.

Conflict – disagreements between people or groups such as a struggle for power or property.

Culture – beliefs, customs and lifestyle of a group of people or a society.

Custom – a way of behaving or an action that is specific to groups of people, a place or a time.

Corps – a combined army unit or group of soldiers who work together. It is pronounced 'core'.

Historian – a person who studies or writes about history.

Memorial – something designed to honour an event, group of people or a person who has died.

Plaques – commemorative plates usually made of metal or wood that are attached to a memorial.

Servicemen and women – men and women who serve in the armed forces.

Symbol – an action, object, event, picture etc that has special meaning and represents something else.

Traditions – beliefs, legends and customs that are handed down from one generation to another.

War correspondent – a person who writes and sends news from places where there are wars .

Index

Bibliography

Australian Army History Unit, *A Brief History of the Australian Army*, Big Sky Publishing, Newport, NSW, 2017.

Conde, A., *A Place to Remember*, Australian War Memorial, Canberra, 2011.

Hopgood, D., *World War I Commemorative Cookbook: A culinary journey through our military history*. Big Sky Publishing, Newport, NSW, 2014.

Paterson, A.M., *Anzac Sons: The Story of Five Brothers in the War to End All Wars*, Big Sky Publishing, Newport, NSW, 2014.

—— *Anzac Sons: Five Brothers on the Western Front*, Big Sky Publishing, Newport, NSW, 2015.

Terrett, L.C. and Taubert S.C., Preserving *Our Proud Heritage: The Customs and Traditions of the Australian Army*, Big Sky Publishing, Newport, NSW, 2011.

Electronic resources

Australian War Memorial website at: www.awm.gov.au

'Remembering Them' App listing war memorials across Australia

ACKNOWLEDGEMENTS

We owe an enormous debt of gratitude to the men and women who have sacrificed so much to serve Australia in times of conflict, both past and present. *Australia Remembers: Anzac Day, Remembrance Day and War Memorials* strives to honour Australian service, presenting a valuable resource for parents and teachers as they impart this country's service legacy to younger generations.

I'd like to express my particular gratitude to the service personnel who gave their time to respond to our call for reflections on what Anzac Day and Remembrance Day mean to them. Many came with stories that touched my heart but were beyond the scope of this book. Thank you for your service and for your voice. Thanks also to the children, all of whom were honoured to contribute their own reflections, and to their parents who granted permission.

My thanks also to Les Terrett and Steve Taubert, the authors of *Preserving Our Proud Heritage: The Customs and Traditions of the Australian Army*, an incredibly detailed Australian Army History Unit compilation published by Big Sky Publishing and the first reference for *Australia Remembers*. In addition, I'd like to thank the research and publications team of the Australian War Memorial for bringing history to life and ensuring its accessibility.

My sincere thanks to Sue Sagar and the staff of St Andrew's Anglican College (Peregian Springs) for their assistance with photos, and to the parents who granted permission for images of their children to be included. I'd like to express my gratitude to Cliff Richards of the Bendigo RSL for putting me in contact with branch photographer, Boyd Robertson, and to Boyd for sorting through images and finding just what I needed. Likewise, my thanks to my parents, Joan and Noel Marlow, my husband Rob and all the children who not only take great photos, but offer enduring encouragement, support and honest comment. To Cath Green who provided the valued and carefully considered review of a respected primary educator and to Dave Elley for the heartening words of an awesome English teacher, I offer my sincere gratitude.

I would like to offer my endless appreciation to Denny Neave, Sharon Evans and Diane Evans at Big Sky Publishing, along with their talented design team, Pat and Chris. Thank you for taking a chance on a very unorthodox and incomplete proposal which you then moulded with care. Your dedication to the preservation of Australia's history is inspirational. Much gratitude also to Cathy McCullagh, a very forgiving and patient editor whose experience, skill and insight is greatly respected and valued.

To my extended family of today and those who came before, thank you. I dedicate this work to Sarah, Charles, Jim, Charlie, George, Allan, Percy and Albert Marlow. As a voice for your descendants, I can truly say we are both proud of and inspired by your courage, dedication, sacrifice and resilience.

To the men and women of the Australian Defence Force — we will not forget.

ABOUT THE AUTHOR

Allison Paterson was a teacher-librarian for over twenty years and has reviewed children's literature for *Magpies Magazine* for almost as long. She was a recipient of a 2017 May Gibbs Children's Literature Trust Creative Time Fellowship. The resulting young adult manuscript **Follow After Me** was published in 2019. Allison now works full-time as a writer, publishing consultant and presenter in schools. She is the author of the 2016 ABIA longlisted and CBCA notable title **Anzac Sons: Five Brothers on the Western Front**, the children's version of her adult non-fiction title **Anzac Sons**. Her children's books include the picture books **Granny's Place**, **Shearing Time**, **I Wonder** and **The Right to Be Me** as well as three books in the highly successful **Australia Remembers** series regarding Australia's military history.

Allison is a Children's Rights Queensland Ambassador. She loves living on the Sunshine Coast where walking on the beach and spending time with her family provide welcome interludes from the desk ... she also welcomes travel, good coffee, cheese and cherry ripes!